D0710307

# Backyard Animals
# Otters

## Kaite Goldsworthy

www.av2books.com

AV² provides enriched content that supplements and complements this book. Weigl's AV² books strive to create inspired learning and engage young minds in a total learning experience.

## Your AV² Media Enhanced books come alive with...

**Audio**
Listen to sections of the book read aloud.

**Key Words**
Study vocabulary, and complete a matching word activity.

**Video**
Watch informative video clips.

**Quizzes**
Test your knowledge.

**Embedded Weblinks**
Gain additional information for research.

**Slide Show**
View images and captions, and prepare a presentation.

**Try This!**
Complete activities and hands-on experiments.

**... and much, much more!**

Go to **www.av2books.com**, and enter this book's unique code.

## BOOK CODE

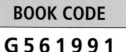

G561991

AV² **by Weigl** brings you media enhanced books that support active learning.

Published by AV² by Weigl
350 5th Avenue, 59th Floor
New York, NY 10118
Website: www.av2books.com    www.weigl.com

Library of Congress Cataloging-in-Publication Data

Goldsworthy, Kaite.
 Otters / Kaite Goldsworthy.
    p. cm. -- (Backyard animals)
 Includes index.
 ISBN 978-1-61690-621-4 (hardcover : alk. paper) -- ISBN 978-1-61690-627-6 (softcover : alk. paper)
 1. Otters--Juvenile literature.  I. Title.
 QL737.C25G65 2011
 599.769--dc22

                              2010045190

Printed in the United States of America in North Mankato, Minnesota
1 2 3 4 5 6 7 8 9 0  15 14 13 12 11

052011
WEP37500

**Editor** Heather Kissock    **Design** Terry Paulhus

# Contents

# Meet the Otter

Otters are **mammals** that spend much of their time in water. Some **species** live in and around oceans. Others live near rivers and lakes. Otters are very good swimmers. They have long bodies and powerful tails that are well-suited to gliding through water. Most species have webbed feet.

The otter is known for its playful nature. Otters can often be seen wrestling or playing tag with each other. Sometimes, they use a riverbank as a slide. They make a path through the mud or snow. Then, they slide down to the water on their backs or bellies.

Otters live in most parts of the world. They can be found on every continent except Australia and Antarctica.

**Fascinating Facts**

Otters communicate using specific noises. These can include clicks, chirps, and squeals. They even have a warning growl.

Otters can swim up to 6 miles (9.66 kilometers) per hour.

# All about Otters

There are 13 species of otter. While they share many features, there are also major differences, especially in size. Northern river otters are about 4 feet (1.2 meters) long. The giant otter, however, can grow to be as long as 6 feet (1.8 m). The Asian small-clawed otter is only about 2 feet (0.6 m) long.

Most otters are semi-aquatic. This means they spend time both in the water and on land. Sea otters live mostly along the Pacific coast of North America. They spend almost their entire life at sea.

Even when on land, otters are usually within 32 yards (30 m) of water.

# Types of Otters

## Eurasian Otter

- Weighs 15 to 22 pounds (7 to 10 kilograms)
- Found in Europe, Asia, and North Africa
- Europe's only otter species

## Sea Otter

- Weighs up to 99 pounds (45 kg)
- Commonly found along the Pacific coast of North America
- Smallest of all **marine mammals**

## Giant Otter

- Weighs about 75 pounds (34 kg)
- Found in South America
- World's largest otter by length

## Asian Small-clawed Otter

- Weighs 2 to 11 pounds (1 to 5 kg)
- Found in Southeast Asia
- Has the smallest claws of all otters

# Otter History

Animals similar to otters have been on Earth for millions of years. Scientists believe that today's otters came from fish-eating animals that lived about five to seven million years ago. Some scientists have found **fossils** from river otters that are 5 to 23 million years old.

At one time, there were hundreds of thousands of otters on Earth. These numbers decreased in the 1700s. People wanted thick otter fur to make coats and hats. Otters were overhunted. Many otter species are now **threatened** as a result. Today, it is against the law to hunt otters in many places.

In the early 1700s, there were almost 300,000 sea otters in the world. Hunting caused the numbers to fall to about 2,000 by the early 1900s.

Sea otters have the thickest fur of any mammal. A male sea otter can have as many as one billion hairs on its body.

# Otter Shelter

Otters live in or very close to water. Most otters have a **den**, or holt, at the water's edge. The dens may be found under a log or in a hollow in the riverbank.

Most dens have an underwater entrance. Inside the den is a large nesting area where the otters rest and raise their young. Many otter species also have a special area on land that they use just for **grooming** and drying their fur.

Sea otters do not have dens. They sometimes rest on rocky shorelines. However, they spend the majority of their lives at sea. They even sleep while floating in the ocean.

## Fascinating Facts

When sleeping, sea otters wrap themselves in seaweed so they do not float away.

Sometimes, otters will use an abandoned beaver den as their home.

# Otter Features

Otters have **adapted** to life in the water. Their **streamlined** bodies and webbed feet help them move through water. Their thick, layered fur keeps them warm and dry.

## FUR

An otter's fur is made up of two coats. The **guard hairs** make up the long outer fur. Short underhairs are found underneath. The two layers trap air between them and help keep the otter dry and warm. Otters must keep their coats very clean to allow the air to be trapped. They spend a large part of the day grooming themselves.

## TAIL

The otter's strong, muscular tail helps it swim and steer through water. An otter uses its tail to balance itself when standing on its back legs. An otter's tail can be up to one third of its body length. The sea otter has a much shorter tail.

## EYES, EARS, AND NOSE

An otter's eyes, ears, and nose are at the top of its head. This allows it to see, hear, and smell while swimming. An otter can close its ears and nose while underwater so that no water gets into them.

## WHISKERS

Otters have whiskers on each side of their head. The whiskers are sensitive to touch and vibrations. They are used to locate **prey** in dark or dirty water.

## FEET

An otter's front paws are shaped like mittens. Most otters have claws that they use to hold on to food. Sea otters can draw their front claws into their paws, much like a cat.

# What Do Otters Eat?

All otters are **carnivores**. Their diets depend on what is available in their **habitat**.

River otters eat mainly fish, but they will also eat reptiles, frogs, small mammals, and birds. Most river otters catch their prey with their mouth.

Sea otters eat fish and marine **invertebrates**, such as clams and crabs. Most of their hunting is done with their front feet.

Most otters have to eat 15 to 25 percent of their body weight in food each day to stay warm. They can spend up to five hours each day searching for food.

Sea otters are one of only a few mammals that use tools. They use rocks to crack open the shells of their prey.

Sea otters eat while floating on their back. They rest their food on their chest.

# Otter Life Cycle

A female otter has her first **litter** when she is five to seven years old. Baby otters are called pups. River otters can have up to six pups in one litter. They give birth to their pups in their den.

## Pups

At birth, otter pups range in size from 4.6 to 7 ounces (130 to 200 grams). Most freshwater otter pups are born helpless and are blind for their first few weeks. Sea otter pups are born with eyes open and a full coat of fur to help them float. All otter pups drink milk from their mother.

## Young Otters

Otter pups learn to swim at about two months old. By four months of age, they can dive and catch food. Pups can be very noisy at this age, squealing loudly so their mother can find them. By six months, most pups can live on their own. They stay with their mother for as long as a year, however. This is when the mother's next litter is born.

Sea otters give birth in the ocean. They usually have only one pup in a season, as they cannot properly care for more.

## Adult

Male sea otters reach adulthood when they are about six years old. Females are considered adults when they are about four years of age. At this time, they begin to mate and have pups of their own. Sea otters usually live 10 to 15 years in nature. However, some can live to be more than 20 years old. The giant otter has a shorter life span. In nature, it lives to be about eight years of age.

# Encountering Otters

Otters are very playful and intelligent animals, but they are also untamed. Wildlife officers advise people to keep a safe distance from otters. An otter that is approached by a human may feel threatened and act out by biting. An otter bite can be dangerous to humans.

Wildlife officers also discourage people from feeding otters. This can make the animal dependent on humans. It will not be able to survive on its own.

If an otter is near, it is best to stay back. If it tries to be friendly, move away from the area until it decides to leave.

## Fascinating Facts

Some otters are nocturnal. This means they are more active at night. Others, such as sea otters, do most of their feeding during the day.

When sea otters grow tired, they join groups and form a raft. Sea otter rafts can be just a few animals or hundreds. Males and females usually form separate rafts.

# Myths and Legends

There are many myths and stories about otters from around the world. American Indians often include otters on their **totem poles** as a symbol of loyalty and trust. Some people even believed that otters were gods in disguise.

In **Celtic** folklore, otters were called "water-dogs" because of their intelligence and playful nature. Scottish stories tell of an "Otter King" who always traveled with seven magical black otters. These otters could grant wishes if they were caught.

Totem poles are found throughout the coastal areas of northwest North America.

# An Otter's Memory

*This is an Ainu legend explaining why otters have trouble remembering things.*

The Ainu are a group of people from Japan. The otter is an important part of many of their legends.

One Ainu legend tells the story of the creation of the first human. The Creator had begun making a human but was called away. He asked an otter to pass a message to one of his helpers. This message explained how the Creator wished humans to be made. The helper was to finish the job. The otter agreed to pass on the message, but became so busy playing in the river and eating fish that he forgot about it. As a result, humans were not created perfectly.

The Creator was so upset with the otter that he took away its memory. Now, otters have trouble remembering.

# Frequently Asked Questions

## Do otters have predators?

**Answer:** Yes. **Predators** are different for each otter species, depending on where it lives. Wolves, cougars, and alligators have been known to eat otters. A sea otter's predators include killer whales, sea lions, and sharks.

## Do otters migrate?

**Answer:** Migration is when animals move from one place to another to find food. Otters do not migrate. They spend most of their life in one area.

## How long can an otter hold its breath?

**Answer:** Otters have very large lungs. These allow otters to hold their breath underwater for up to eight minutes.

# Words to Know

**adapted:** adjusted to the natural environment

**carnivores:** animals that eat other animals

**Celtic:** relating to a group of ancient peoples who lived in western Europe and the British Isles

**den:** an animal's home

**fossils:** the hardened remains of animals or plants that lived long ago

**grooming:** cleaning fur, hair, or skin to remove dirt

**guard hairs:** long, coarse hairs that protect softer hairs underneath

**habitat:** the environment in which an animal lives

**invertebrates:** animals that do not have a backbone

**litter:** a group of baby animals born together

**mammals:** warm-blooded animals that have a spine, fur or hair, and drink milk from their mother

**marine mammals:** warm-blooded animals that live in water

**predators:** animals that hunt other animals for food

**prey:** an animal that is hunted

**species:** animals or plants that share certain features and can breed together

**streamlined:** designed to move smoothly through water

**threatened:** a group of animals or plants that is at risk of disappearing

**totem poles:** logs that have been carved and painted with emblems

# Index

# Log on to www.av2books.com

AV² by Weigl brings you media enhanced books that support active learning. Go to www.av2books.com, and enter the special code found on page 2 of this book. You will gain access to enriched and enhanced content that supplements and complements this book. Content includes video, audio, web links, quizzes, a slide show, and activities.

**Audio**
Listen to sections of the book read aloud.

**Video**
Watch informative video clips.

**Embedded Weblinks**
Gain additional information for research.

**Try This!**
Complete activities and hands-on experiments.

# WHAT'S ONLINE?

| Try This! | Embedded Weblinks | Video | EXTRA FEATURES |
|---|---|---|---|
| Identify different types of otters. | More information on identification. | Watch a video about otter behavior. | **Audio** Listen to sections of the book read aloud. |
| List important features of the otter. | More information on the history of otters. | See an otter in its natural environment. | **Key Words** Study vocabulary, and complete a matching word activity. |
| Compare the similarities and differences between young and adult otters. | Complete an interactive activity. | | |
| Test your knowledge of otters. | More information on encountering otters. | | **Slide Show** View images and captions, and prepare a presentation. |
| | More stories and legends. | | **Quizzes** Test your knowledge. |

AV² was built to bridge the gap between print and digital. We encourage you to tell us what you like and what you want to see in the future.
**Sign up to be an AV² Ambassador at www.av2books.com/ambassador.**